How to Have an Asian Fetish
by Angelina Zhang

© 2015 by Angelina Zhang

How to Have an Asian Fetish

Intro

Asian Fetishes are a status symbol. It's not even the Asian girlfriend in your bed, the Chinese character tattoo on your bicep, or the Naruto collection on your shelf that is the status symbol. It's the fetish itself that gives you status. You either have an Asian fetish or desperately wish you had one. What BMWs, Polo shirts, and espresso makers were for previous ages, the Asian fetish is for today. You can't make it big without an Asian fetish. Just look at Nicolas Cage, Larry Ellison, Wesley Snipes, or John Lennon! Asian fetishes have been bringing it since the sixties, but especially now.

Like any status symbol, an Asian Fetish must be carefully acquired, groomed, and even maintained. It's not something to be taken lately. And as difficult as it is to "do" an Asian Fetish properly, it's also monumentally difficult to find the right advice. Ask a fellow fetishist whether you should listen to Kpop or Jpop, or whether you should masturbate to Lucy Liu in *Charlie's Angels* or to Zhang Ziyi in *Crouching Tiger Hidden Dragon*, and you might intentionally be led astray.

This book is your must-read guide for knowing all about Asian fetishes. I leave no corner unexplored. No sub-fetish unmentioned. No lock of silky black hair uncarressed. I'll lovingly guide you through the world of Asian fetishes, using every last bit of my deep, intensive, throbbing experience as a real-life Asian girl.

I'm inscrutable, seductive, gentle, and ferocious. As I sweep back that silky long jet-black hair, I can declare one thing to you -- demurely, of course -- I know my Asian fetishes! I don't just collect or analyze Asian fetish. I curate them. I celebrate them. Am I offended by them? No way. I'm offended only when they're done wrong or not properly maintained.

What's Asian fetish disaster? I once walked in on my boyfriend sitting on the couch with his Ipad propped up on the pillow, his boxers around his knees, his hand on his tool, and a photo montage of Selena Gomez flying across the screen as my beloved's hand flew back-and-forth across his johnson. The problem here is not that my boyfriend was masturbating. The problem is that, as he confessed, he believed this was an Asian girl he was masturbating to. There was no name on the photo montage. She has dark hair. She has something of that prized exotic look. It's a mistake anyone could make. But thanks to *this* book, it's a mistake you, dear reader, never will make.

Another Asian fetish disaster? A guy once messaged me on a dating website. His message was written in English. He didn't compliment me on my almond-shaped eyes or on my honey-colored skin. He didn't tell me about his favorite kind of chow mein. He didn't ask me if I want to go to his place to see his collection of ben-wa balls. Fail. Don't let this happen to you. Read this book.

First principles of the Asian fetish

Edward Said famously wrote in *Orientalism* that "From the beginning of Western speculation about the Orient, the one thing the Orient could not do was to represent itself." "The Orient," Said continued, "is watched, since its almost (but never quite) offensive behavior issues out of a reservoir of infinite peculiarity."

That's some heavy stuff. And it's correct. After all, having attended Harvard, Edward Said is an expert on Asian fetishes. Asian fetishism has been a requirement for entry into Ivy League schools for at least the past twenty years, and even in Said's time, it was highly recommended. I've seen the Harvard student brochures. Every section about ethnic diversity shows a white guy posing happily with an Asian girl. Here "diversity" of course means that some Asian fetishes favor Korean girls while others favor Chinese girls, while all hold out in unrequited hopeful desire for the ever-elusive Japanese girl.

But we don't need fancy book learning to know that we Orientals are infinitely peculiar and more or less can't represent ourselves. Did you need to read a book before you knew Asian girls are hot? Probably not. That's common knowledge. As common knowledge as these universally accepted first principles of the Asian fetish:

1. Whatever your deficiencies in the eyes of your native culture and society, and especially in the eyes of the women of your native culture and society, those deficiencies are strengths -- not just strengths, but objects of intense adoration and catnip-induced mewing with desire -- for Asian culture and especially for Asian chicks. In Asia, a pot belly is a sign of wisdom. In Asia, a bald head is a sign of good fortune. In Asia, poverty is a sign of virtue. In Asia, domestic violence is a sign of marital harmony. And so on.

2. Asian chicks never sweat, shit, or fart, except in the specialized genres of Japanese porn dedicated to those activities.

3. Evil porcupine-legged softball-playing feminism never made it to Asia. Asian women know that the proper role of a

woman is to provide her man with sandwiches and fellatio. It's not sexist!!! It's just the natural order.

4. Asian societies are free of conflict (except kung-fu fighting scenes), rebellion (except when your girlfriend bravely dates you against her evil parents' wishes), or hooliganism and social loutism (except Asian men).

5. Asian men are woefully inadequate in all regards, have penises unnoticed by anyone lacking an electron-scanning microscope, and lead bitter lives as kung-fu masters or accountants, either way, beating their wives and children whenever possible, and crying about their small penises all the way. This all contributes to the Asian mystique.

We can all agree on this much.

My first experience with the Asian fetish

I was a university student in Shanghai around the year 2000. I was studying "international economics," which in a Chinese university, just means "how to export cheap factory goods to foreign companies." Despite the "international" subject matter of my education, this point in my life, I'd never directly interacted with a non-Chinese person -- much less a white person -- in my life. I had seen some "foreigners" (my generic mental category at that time for anyone not Han Chinese like me) on the street and in public places and tourist sites around Shanghai, but had not even entertained the idea that one could actually interact with them. To me up until then, they were like characters in a tv show: they're fun to watch, but don't expect them to react to you or even be aware of you.

And at that time, we heard rumblings among the students, that there was going to be a "laowai" (foreigner, usually white) instructor in our department sometime in the future. And that he (we just assumed such an instructor would be male, which turned out true) would be teaching a course, only for the advanced students of international economics. And that he was handsome. How did these tidbits leak out to us students? I have no idea. I can tell you, however, that unlike the case in a first-world university, in a Chinese university, the students have no advance knowledge of what classes are going to be available to them, what instructors are being hired, or even when the school year will begin an end. Any such news is more or less announced at the last second, and students are expected to deal with it. And asking for information from official university sources would lead not only to a lack of answers, but to an accusation of being badly behaved or something. So the rumors circulated, without official confirmation or disconfirmation.

Before the start of the following semester, rumors number one and two were confirmed: there was indeed a laowai instructor, and he would be teaching a course. We had no idea what the course would be about. Definitely something foreigner-ish. Maybe Western trade. Maybe dollars. Maybe basketball. Or cheeseburgers. Would we be interested in taking the class? Here we divided into two distinct groups -- risk-seeking and risk-averse. Still having no idea what the course was about, nor much about our instructor-to-be, about half of my cohort was intensely interested in taking the class, while the other half was intensely terrified. The division went fairly well along with the division of those who were generally more risk-seeking, or even thrill-seeking.

Can you guess which group I was in?

Right.

I told the registration office that I wanted to sign up for the class. Which class? "That one class!" I told them. As if everyone knew. And they did know. "The one with the foreign teacher?" Yes, yes, a million times yes!

Was I engaging in a non-Asian fetish here? Not really. I didn't have any expectations of that specific foreigner. Just a desire to experience something different. Had there been a Japanese or Martian or transsexual instructor, I would've been equally eager.

The class turned out to be, predictably enough, about English-language marketing. Keep in mind: at this time in China's economic development, the "best," or really only, industry to be in was selling manufactured goods to the first world. And in our minds at that time, everyone in the first world spoke English. So it was going to be exactly the class we needed. And exactly the kind of class we were quite confident our instructors couldn't teach us. The problem turned out to be that this teacher couldn't either.

A decently high score on our internal university English exam was a prerequisite for taking the class. Check. Actually, that requirement made the class more gender-balanced than normally a business class would be. The business student body as a whole was probably 75% male. But for whatever reason, the girls were better at learning English. And the girls were also more eager to try a new instructor and class. So this class was about half male half female. And I was in it. Was I ever!

Our instructor entered class the first day, and came up to the chalkboard. He looked just like every other "laowai" foreigner we'd ever imagined. Tall, pasty-skinned, chubby, with light brown hair. As far as our age estimates of Westerners went, he could've been 25 or 55. He was from Foreignerland, somewhere out there -- Canada, I later learned. Maybe I should have known what things were about when his first greeting was to address a group of girls sitting together and say in almost awkwardly too-slow-and-clear English, "Ni hau ma, beautiful ladies!" I was one of those beautiful ladies. And we were not flattered but terrified and embarrassed of this attention. At the time, I reasoned that this was normal behavior in a Western classroom.

In fact, my classmates and I dismissed all his peculiarities as "that's just how foreigners are." Or "that's normal in foreigners' culture." (Foreigners' culture: a homogenous monolith!) And when Mr. G always put his arm around me when I visited his office, and always liked to inspect the necklace I was wearing that day (that necklace hanging at a scenic viewpoint of course), I also dismissed it as "Well now I know how life is in foreign universities! The teachers are very affectionate with students!" In fact, he expressed unmistakeable sexual interest in the female students, starting from the first few days of class.

But being a lecher isn't the same as having an Asian fetish. If that were true, you wouldn't need this book, only a trenchcoat and some high-quality j/o lube. My introduction to the Asian-fetish angle is when Mr. G explicitly disavowed what had up to that point been our mental model: that this behavior was normal in the Western first world. I was standing in Mr. G's office one day, and as he usually did, he put his arm around me as he talked with me. Again: I thought that was normal where he came from, perhaps because I'd seen couples doing exactly in movies, and I hadn't realized that what's normal for couples in the first world is not normal for professors and students.

And as he had his arm around me, he started telling me, in the form of a supposed compliment, "You know, back in Canada, people wouldn't allow us to hug like this, but China doesn't have those hangups." I didn't quite know what a "hangup" is, but I was so shocked by the first part of his sentence that I asked him to explain what he meant. And he said that in the West, women have been keeping men constrained, and not allowing them to express themselves, and in the West, it would be considered improper for a male professor to embrace his female students. Wow. This was news. Worldview-changing news.

As impervious as Mr. G was to social cues, he didn't pick up on my shock to what he'd told me. Instead, he told me that he strongly preferred Chinese women to Western women, because Chinese women didn't have "hangups." We did have internet in the university library then, and I couldn't wait to go to an internet terminal and check what exactly "hangups" are. I did do that immediately after that revelational meeting -- his office was next to the library anyway -- and found that it meant that we Chinese girls had no moral limits, or something like that.

And what happened then with Mr. G? Due to our lack of "hangups," we, his female students, hosted Mr. G for a three-hole ten-way interracial gangbang in the girls' dormitory, immediately after evening Mao Zedong recitations. Then, our almond eyes agape and horizontal vaginas puckered in ecstasy, we decided to abandon the "international marketing" facade of the class, and just make it "interracial gangbang." Let's just say I got an A+.

Actually, we, his students, were intrigued but mildly offended. And Mr. G's insistence to making us fit his Oriental fantasies, rather than our reality, continued in our actual classwork. In teaching us international marketing, Mr. G seemed to assume that all of us lived in a kung fu movie or a children's storybook. For example, when introducing to us the concept of brand loyalty, Mr. G started off assuming that branding would be a tremendously difficult thing for us Orientals to understand, and went on a roundabout metaphor about brand loyalty being like "family honor" and something about Confucius (who, unbeknownst to Mr. G, was more or less forbidden in China in those days) and then gave us a look that said "I know you still don't understand, but maybe if I repeat more of my brilliant metaphors, you'll understand?" He had no idea that all of us were pretty brand-obsessed, and also that the concept of product branding most likely originated in China.

Mr. G's classroom lectures often veered into his discussions of what he thought was wrong with the world, or at least with Canada. What we had expected from a foreign teacher was digressions about why his home country is better than China. We had assumed that definitely to a foreigner's eyes, and also perhaps to objective eyes (ours!), foreign countries were far superior to China -- please remember that this story happened still some years before China's meteoric economic rise and renewed sense of ultra-nationalistic pride. Instead, we were often treated to a lecture, only vaguely related to marketing, where Part 1 described some unpleasant experience in Mr. G's life back in Canada, Part 2 generalized that unpleasant experience to some flaw Mr. G perceived in

Canada or in Western society, and Part 3 told us that China was mercifully free of that flaw.

Mr. G, an expert on China having lived there since the beginning of that semester, told us that China was free of: feminism, picky or demanding women, laziness, insubordination, high prices, taxes, anti-smoking campaigns, divorce, and government corruption. He was certainly having a honeymoon period. It was refreshing for us to hear all this, as Mr. G's complaints about Canada were in most ways comfortingly similar to our own parents' and uncles' and aunts' complaints about China. But Mr. G had thought that in his ideal China, there's nothing like, for example, a rude shop clerk or a lazy employee or a lying girlfriend.

As you might expect, many of Mr. G's bugaboos concerned women specifically. And just as he'd found an ideal country (in his mind, after a few weeks of residency) in China, so he'd found the ideal woman in his naive female students. It was not difficult to be asked on a dinner date by Mr. G. Almost any conversation in his office between Mr. G and a female student (Maybe with male students too? Not that there's anything wrong with that!) ended with an invitation to tea or dinner to discuss the matter more in depth.

It was during those dinner dates when the conversation moved to romantic matters, and again to all the reasons we Chinese girls were better than those evil, hairy-legged, softball-playing, Subaru-driving (no, I didn't know that joke at the time) Canadian girls. As far as Mr. G saw, we Chinese girls weren't concerned with money or status. That is perhaps the most false thing I've heard all my life. But anyway, according to Mr. G, back in Canada, women weren't very interested in him, because he lived in a small apartment, didn't have a car, and only worked as a high-school substitute teacher. (How did this guy become a "professor" in China, you ask? It was pretty common at the time in China to assume any white person is highly qualified in anything. Mr. G could have probably been doing open-heart surgery in a Chinese hospital had he claimed to be an expert.) And here in China, he had women falling all over him, because he was such a great guy, and Chinese women didn't care about silly things like money or status.

If you have ever met a Chinese woman, or seen a photo of a Chinese woman, or met someone who's met a Chinese woman, or been in a room with a Chinese woman, you would know that money and status is pretty much all Chinese women care about in a potential mate. Of course Mr. G was so popular with the ladies in China not because they were deeply attuned to his higher human qualities, but because they saw his white skin, Canadian citizenship, and job as a university instructor as marks of high status.

In addition to Chinese women's supposed higher values of appreciating and loving men like Mr. G, there was also quite a bit we were told about our beautiful slim figures, our short statures (he intended this as a compliment), and of course our "almond eyes." (I and most of my classmates had never heard the word "almond" in English until we started sharing tales of Mr. G talking about "almond-shaped eyes," just as we'd never heard the term "hangups" until we'd listened to Mr. G describing Canadian women.) We weren't that surprised, because we'd heard that foreigners had different beauty standards from our own, although it was still amusing to hear it. He of course had no idea that we all wanted to be taller and have rounder eyes, and that while we liked being slim, many of our parents had directly experienced famines and starvation.

I was intrigued by Mr. G, because he was the first foreigner I'd ever met, and despite his weirdnesses, it was flattering to catch the attention and the compliments of a foreigner. But I didn't get any farther with him than a few dinner and tea shop meetings, after which he invariably asked if I wanted to see a certain book of his at his apartment, and to which I'd politely responded that I had to go back to the dorm and study. (Wow, I guess we Chinese girls have hangups too!)

I'm pretty sure Mr. G had sex with at least a few of my classmates, and even more of my university-mates. I didn't have any solid information, but he was working so hard at it, and asking girls left and right, that it had to have happened, even if only by sheer luck or the law of large numbers. I can only imagine what such a sexual encounter must have been like. Maybe it involved a discussion of how evil Western women make him use a condom, or refuse to swallow his semen, but perfect Chinese girls are happy with bareback bukkake fests. Or something like that. But in any case, it must have only reinforced Mr. G's preconceptions (most of which were self-confirming anyway!), and it certainly didn't dissuade him from pursuing more and more of that delicious Chinese poon.

What larger conclusions can we draw from this solitary experience of Mr. G? And how can this story help you cultivate your own Asian fetish? After all, this is just the story of one slightly cartoonish and definitely buffoonish Canadian man trying to be a playboy in China some fifteen years ago. The whole experience is personally memorable for me, because it was my first brush with Asian fetishes, but it's also generally instructive for what I want to tell you about the proper creation and cultivation of your Asian fetish.

It was easy to see the process of fetishization with Mr. G because he did it toward the whole country of China (or maybe just "Asia" in his mind), not only toward specific women. He discussed his thought process openly. He didn't hide. I don't remember now, but maybe at the time, he also told us how back in Canada, women would reject him for having an Asian fetish, but not so in China.

We didn't reject him for having an Asian fetish. In fact, we didn't consider it a fetish, but a strong interest in and appreciation of our culture, which we liked. We did think he completely misunderstood us and our culture, but that was about as much as we had expected of a foreigner. What we didn't expect is that in place of correctly understanding us, he placed not blame, but projections of how he wished his home country, and that country's women, would be. Somehow his lack of understanding resulted not in negative evaluations of us, but positive (to him) evaluations. Everywhere he saw a blank spot -- something he knew nothing about, or only had a hunch about -- he filled in his wishful thinking about what kind of place he wants to live in, or how he wants the world to be. You know, we all love to believe untruths that are particularly comfortable to believe. And indeed we choose the most comfortable and fulfilling ones. So when Mr. G moves to a new place, what untruth more comfortable than that he's finally found a place that appreciates him, and that women are throwing themselves at him not because they're desperate to emigrate, but because they are so enlightened and so attuned to his higher ideals!

It's a little bit like the well-known story about the foreigner who marries a Chinese woman. In the beginning, she doesn't know English, and he doesn't know Chinese, and whenever he is speaking English, she imagines him to be saying wonderful things, and whenever she is speaking Chinese, he imagines her to be saying wonderful things. And the marriage is perfect and happy. But then she learns English or he learns Chinese, and everything falls apart, because they finally confront the reality of their real feelings, and not what they imagine themselves to have been saying.

If you believe in heaven, what do you imagine it's like? If you love dogs, you imagine heaven being full of dogs. If you hate dogs, I'm pretty sure you imagine heaven is a no-dog zone. Either way, it's your ideal. And you've presumably never visited heaven (not talking about the feeling of a deep-throat BJ) so your imagine pretty much runs unrestrained. And moreover, maybe whatever traits of yours you believe are not appreciated in your current life, you imagine would be appreciated in heaven -- isn't that in fact the very idea of heaven, a place where you'll be rewarded for actions or qualities that maybe hold little reward in earthly life? I'm sorry to get theological here, but the comparison is I think a really good one, because when I hear white guys (ones who don't know much about Asia or Asians) talking about Asian girls, or about Asia in general, it sounds just like a Christian talking about heaven.

We Asians tend to catch whatever nice dreams our particular imaginers and conjurers might have. To go back to Edward Said, Asia is a geographical continent, but "the Orient" is a canvas on which people paint their fantasies.

Just like ideas of heaven, ideas of the ideal mate conflict. That's why we Asian girls are innocent and lascivious all in the same breath, in the fetishist's mind.

What you should learn from this is that it's completely ok to have contradictory standards within your standard of the perfect Asian wife or even the perfect Asian wall painting. And if your friends disagree about whether Asian girls are prudish or slutty? The correct answer is not "Asian girls are individuals, and vary just as any individuals would." The correct answer: "man, is heaven hot or cold? all depends on your ideal, right?"

Fetish and where to swing it: practical advice

We all know that you believe Asia to be beautiful and terrible and Asian women to be virginal and slutty, but what good is a falling tree if no one hears it? What good is your Asian fetish if no one finds out about it? Would John Holmes's penis have been worth anything had he not starred in porn? Of course not.

If you're a college student -- and college is the birthplace of many Asian fetishes -- the opportunities for proudly exhibiting your fetish are nearly infinite. Most obviously, you can use your college major to display your prized fetish. East Asian Culture or Chinese or Japanese Language are excellent choices, and show off your special proclivity, much as John Holmes's film oeuvre showed off his special you-know-what. You are also likely to meet Chinese or Japanese chicks who are looking for an easy thing to major in. However, you have to be careful on this one, and don't check the form or click the box as soon as you see the word "Asian" and "studies." There's a big snake in the grass, waiting to lunge out at you. That snake is called Asian-American studies, and its venom is called feminism. Do not, for any reason, under any circumstance, major or even go anywhere near Asian-American Studies, because it's full of hairy-legged feminists, and is exactly not the kind of environment where you can indulge your love for pure, virginal prime-grade, nubile, unsoiled Asian… culture. In fact, around Asian-American Studies departments you are likely to find, beside old copies of Giant Robot and the collected works of Frank Chin, a serious prejudice and even hatred toward Asian fetishes and the people who have them. They might dress up in white-hooded kimonos and burn a joss stick on your lawn. Watch out.

Unlike hairy-legged Asian-American Studies departments, super-cute, kawaii anime clubs are an excellent home for cultivating Asian fetishism. Fortunately, the population overlap between an anime club and an Asian-American studies department is always exactly zero. Unfortunately, the population overlap between the anime club and Asian girls who weigh under 200 pounds is also pretty much zero. But all in stride, grasshopper.

Majored in East Asian Studies, joined the anime club, and still want more? If you're ready for true master-level fetishism, I present to you the coup de grace: joining the Asian Students' Association. As a non-Asian. This is a heroic move. You'll be the next Bruce Jenner. You will be guaranteeing yourself a steady flow of Asian... culture in your life. And quite a few quizzical looks. Of course explain to anyone who asks that you're very, very, extremely interested in Asian... culture. Bring some fortune cookies to break the ice. A few back issues of your uncle's collection of *Oriental Dolls* wouldn't hurt either.

Depending on your particular college's composition, upon joining the Asian Students' Association, you could either be swimming balls-deep in warm, moist "culture" that very evening, or just be subject to a lot of quizzical looks. And that of course depends on whether most people in the Asian students' club are beautiful pure unmolested specimens freshly arrived from most likely China, or whether they are filthy adulterated American-born specimens. Which group is likely to love your fetish, and which is likely to treat you like a fucking freak? For now, we'll leave that question as an exercise for the curious reader, but we'll explore it further in the invaluable chapter about taking your Asian fetish on the road.

Speaking of "on the road": colleges, unlike workplaces, offer international travel (wink, wink, nudge nudge) opportunities to pretty much everyone. Popular destinations for studying abroad include Japan, China, Japan, Japan, China, and Japan. Seize the opportunity. Even if your major is something decidedly non-fetishistic, like, say, mathematics, loudly proclaim that you are interested in *pure* mathematics, and of course everything in Asia is *pure*, ergo you must spend a semester in Japan.

If any of that fails, don't ignore the potential of mass-marketing. Big business does it, so why can't big fetish do it too? Here's the key. Get your college's student directory, if it is possible to obtain one printed on paper, and go to the hotbeds of potential prospects in the alphabetical listing of surnames: the Ch's, the Li's, the Ng's, the Zh's. Eliminate any surname that is more than one syllable long (this method will eliminate chicks who hail from Thailand-Philippines, but that is because you're saving them until your golden years). If you're technologically minded, you can write a Python script for this. And eliminate any too male-sounding first names, unless, of course, you swing that way. Then call them up. Or knock on their dorm room door. Or Facebook friend them. And say that you need help with your assignment on Asian culture or almond eyes or Audrey Hepburn or whatever. Instant goldmine. Or exotic-green-jade-mine, as it were.

The ones with Anglo-sounding first names, you should be wary of. They may consider themselves to be "Americans just like you." (LOL) They may even be members of an Asian-American group and sit around reading old issues of Giant Robot. Danger, danger. Unless they have deep tans and complaint about how they "would, like, never date an Asian guy, yuck," they may not appropriately appreciate yoru Asian fetish. That's ok. You can find better, more authentic, certainly more exotic Asian specimens by iterating the first search method: just focus on those whose first name, as well as their last name has the magical Ch or Li or Ng or Zh. Pure gold. Or jade.

But what if you're beyond college, and in the working world, and you want to cultivate an Asian fetish -- either one acquired during college, or a relatively new one? In the adult world, your pure virginal perfect Asian specimens are not going to be handed to you on a jade-lined platter as they would be in college. But definitely don't despair, because a post-college professional has myriad actionable opportunities to leverage Asian fetishism to produce synergistic deliverables. Which means, you too can be a fetishist, and you too can catch the yellowtail, even if you're way beyond the stocked fishing pond that is college.

As an adult, you have an important choice to make here. It might well be the choice that determines the path of your fetish cultivation. And that choice is whether to live in the San Francisco Bay Area, Los Angeles, or somewhere else?

San Francisco used to be known as the capital of gay culture, back when being gay was hip and cutting-edge. Now that gay people are known to include your underarm-stained geography teacher and your fat racist uncle, gay fetishism is out of fashion in San Francisco. Asian fetishism is in. Asian is the new gay. You used to show off your gay friend, but now you show off your Asian girlfriend, or at least your Asian love interest, or at least your collection of sake glasses or chopsticks. I mean, *The Joy Luck Club* was set in San Francisco! There's an entire Asian Art Museum in San Francisco, built exclusively to give Asian fetishists a place to go on dates! San Francisco is even the home of the most well-known website built exclusively for white men to find Asian women: Craigslist. What more could you want?

Not so fast. There are three big problems with cultivating your Asian fetish in San Francisco.

The first problem is that you can forget about being unique. It's like going to Waikiki to cultivate your image as a surfer. Sure, it's the center of surfing culture, but every other dude is a surfer too. And so it is with San Francisco, except every other guy in your overpriced and run-down Victorian apartment house is also desperately trying to surf Asian some Asian pussy. This leads not only to competition for the aforementioned pussy (meow!), but a lack of status and distinction. In Suwanee, Georgia, you can parade your Asian fetish around, because it's the only one on the block. In San Francisco, it's welcome to the Asian fetish club, you and every guy at your office and also your dad and also your twelve-year-old nephew.

The second problem, perhaps deadlier, is the huge Asian population of San Francisco places you at risk of losing your fetish. The literature on Asian fetishes is rife with tragic stories of young bucks who moved to San Francisco to cultivate an Asian fetish, and after a few mornings packed on a bus between five vinegar-smelling sweaty aunties screaming at each other in Taishanese, those once-promising young bucks lose the plot. They start thinking Asian people are just like anyone else. They even stop believing that Asian women are the solution for all their problems. It's been proven: exposure to fleshy, smelly specimens of Asian femininity carries a strong danger of exploding fetishistic ideals, at least if you, my dear fetishist, get too close. And the big problem in San Francisco is that you stand a very real risk, in San Francisco, of getting way too close.

Sure, you can hang out in the parts of San Francisco that protect you from being triggered in this manner. The latest Asian-fusion bistro in the Marina District is likely to be full of Asian women experienced in helping you improve yourself and cultivate your fetish -- with long straight black hair, deep tans, cheongsam-style blouses, and tales of their previous boyfriends Chad and Blake. So is the Asian Art Museum, and, mercifully, even hipster hangouts in the Mission. But get too close to some housewares store on a back alley in the Richmond District, and your world might fall apart, with nary a Suzie Wong haircut or a floral cheongsam in sight -- and instead, a bunch of, say, old men and women eating pig offal porridge, speaking in dialects that have no semblance of "ni hao ma?" and having absolutely no interest in your adorable attempts at studying traditional calligraphy.

The third potential problem may be the deadliest. What do you think happened to everyone who majored in Asian American Studies back in college? The ones who gave you snickers or dirty looks as you were rushing to anime club meetings embracing your inflatable Japanese lolita girlfriend? The ones who were all, like, AZN STRONG? They didn't dissolve in their own bile. And not all of them went to work for Gawker. What happened to most of them: they moved to San Francisco. For reals. In the Mission District and Tenderloin, you are going to find militant Asian-American feminists who are going to bash your head in for offering to teach them English, before you can even begin to say "it's just a preference." And with your head bashed in, you won't even be able to comment on their almond eyes.

These kinds of dangerous urban-warfare encounters are exactly why you should seriously consider living in Los Angeles. Yes, Los Angeles is also full of those not so fetish-friendly Asians, including a huge population of gun-toting Korean grocers who might feed you lead if you look at their daughters and your BMW isn't at least a 5-series. But, speaking of BMWs, here's the good thing about Los Angeles: cars. Roads, Car culture. Physical separation between *you* and *what you don't want to see*. Does Los Angeles have auntie-jeans-wearing Chinese aunties who don't have tans and don't read Amy Tan? Absolutely. Do you ever have to see them? No. Never. Stay out of certain area codes, such as 626, and you'll be safe. It's as if the whole city had a number-coded trigger warning system. Don't want to be triggered -- and don't want to risk losing your Asian fetish religion? The numbers 626 and 949 are your trigger warnings, as is the numeric-alphanumeric codeword *99 Ranch*. Stay away from those and you mercifully are unlikely to be triggered.

Want to carefully exercise and nourish your Asian fetish? If you already have an Asian girlfriend, rent an apartment in Silverlake with her, and rave about how racially inclusive you are. If you are looking for an

Asian girlfriend, or just want to admire pure Asian beauty, the Santa Monica Promenade is your spot to gaze lovingly at virginal, innocent Asian female specimens just prime for the picking every weekend morning, as soon as they've cleaned up from the previous night's club encounter. Long straight black hair is guaranteed. Or, if you prefer fishing in a stocked pond, do what Nicolas Cage did, and go to a hostess club in Koreatown, where you are literally guaranteed, as in money-back guaranteed, to find an adoring long-black-haired maiden who never says "no."

And while Asian fetishes aren't rare in Los Angeles, they're just one fetish in a sea of many. So you likely won't be one of a hundred single dudes in your condo building with an Asian fetish. You will enjoy some degree of uniqueness. But you'll have to compete with people with scat fetishes, cuck fetishes, giantess fetishes, whatever. That could be heady competition. In fact, an Asian fetish is, in Los Angeles, a tad bit boring. You'll be accepted, but you won't be getting the red-carpet invites just because of your Thai-script tattoo and your collection of zen green tea.

Want to go where an Asian fetish is really unusual and highly respected? Pretty much anywhere outside coastal U.S. cities will be good for you. Sit down at a Starbucks in, say, Suwanee, Georgia, take out your manga comics collection, put it next to your Chinese calligraphy textbook, sip your green tea latte, and browse your filtered search results (Gender=female, Race=Asian, Virgin=yes). You'll be the only one doing that. And because of the general dearth of Asians there, you are somewhat unlikely to find an unshaved Korean auntie or Asian-American feminist to blast your fetishizing into outer space.

If you live outside the major coastal cities of the U.S., celebrating your fetish with a suitable Asian female target is going to be more difficult than just strolling into an LA K-Town hostess club was for Mr. Cage or going to Harvard was for Mr. Zuckerberg. There is, however, one method that is the tried-and-true go-to method for all Asian fetishists, whether in California, middle America, or even in Asia. You likely know it already. It's called: *language exchange.* It's the battle boast and mating call of the Asian fetishist. (In fact, when I was a college student in China, it was the mating call of the foreigner fetishist.)

College billboards and local websites, including Craigslist, are great places for posting an ad for language exchange. To avoid disappointment, make sure you emphasize that you want to learn only Asian languages, and only from native speakers, female ones. And which Asian language? You don't care, really, though Hebrew might be a stretch.

Once you get a reply to your ad for language exchange, make sure to ask your exchange partner the right questions to ensure that she's qualified for linguistic education. Age? Relationship status? Is she available for in-home language exchange? And so on. In fact, emphasize that you're pretty flexible about the language part, as far as the other criteria are fulfilled.

When I first arrived in the United States, I was on a student visa, studying at a community college in Los Angeles. I had already obtained my college degree in China, but I wanted to experience an American college and practice using English. My boyfriend at the time (a white American whom I'd met in China) lived in New York, but I was more interested in living in Los Angeles (after all, it's Hollywood!), especially when I found out that it would be significantly cheaper to live in Los Angeles than New York.

I had heard about language exchange. In fact, I had furtively tried to do language exchange -- or tried to just "talk to foreigners" -- in Shanghai, without much success. And so when I saw at my community college billboard an ad for free language exchange -- English and Chinese or Japanese -- I thought I'd struck gold. And in fact, I had struck gold, in that the "Chinese or Japanese" was the mark (unbeknownst to me at the time) of an Asian fetish. The ad might as well have said "Chinese or Japanese or Korean or Thai or Mongolian or whatever the Asian chix are speaking these days."

My language exchange partner, Jack (that *was* his real name, unfortunately not uncommon enough to justify me changing it here), replied to my furtively written email by spilling out a few paragraphs, what I would now know to call a "wall of text," about how glad he was to have found a language exchange partner. He even mentioned that he would treat me with respect and caring, unlike Chinese men, to whom he believed respect and caring were unknown concepts. I did have a flashback to Mr. G, my university instructor in Shanghai, and I was just waiting for Jack to tell me about how much better Chinese women are than white women.

Which he did, at our first meeting. In fact, he told me that his white female classmates are all sluts (using that word), and that he could see from just looking at me that I'm a virgin. Which I most definitely was not. But, of course, in his mind, I was pure, unspoiled, and most importantly, Asian, so of course I was a virgin. Just as according to Mr. G, I must not have any "hangups." And the way Jack was staring at me when we first met made me think he really *was* a virgin, and reminded me of the Chinese mythical character of the "color wolf," the "horny goat" equivalent in Chinese mythology, a wolf who is so overcome with sexual passion that phosphoresces a rainbow of colors.

Of course when Jack and I went to "do language exchange," there was little discussion of language, and a lot of discussion about me, my relationship status, and my dating history. In fact, it was reminiscent of the dates I used to have with my high school boyfriend, when we claimed to be "practicing English," but really were spending time together -- with the difference being, the high school version was by mutual consent, while this was something that I really wanted to be only language exchange. When I told Jack that I have a boyfriend, he assumed that my boyfriend is Chinese (not true) and mentioned something about him having a tiny dick (definitely not true) and of course being boorish and abusive (ridiculously not true). And, almost as a matter of obligation, when Jack and I left the restaurant and were standing on the sidewalk outside, he tried to kiss me.

It takes a woman better than I am to appreciate such an advanced level of Asian fetishism. I wish I could have embraced the strength, purity, and relentlessness of Jack's Asian fetish. But instead, I was just annoyed that he seemed more interested in dating me than in helping me with English. And from then on, I took a strong lead, and said we'd meet at a library study room, and specifically focus only on language exchange. I also suggested that I would bring one of my male Chinese friends with me to join the language exchange. Well, either Jack's Asian fetish didn't extend to MMF interracial threesomes, or somehow my ideas didn't fit his fetish. So that was it with Jack. And I found that "language exchange" was such a hot bed of beautifully unrestrained Asian fetishism -- I foolishly thought limiting it to "female only" would help, but I only encountered lesbian Asian fetishists -- that I decided to just learn English the regular way, through regular informal conversations in and around my school.

If you haven't yet posted an ad offering language exchange, post one now. Write it on a page torn out of this book if you must. But one simply cannot have an Asian fetish without being somehow involved in language exchange. Bonus points if you never mention which Asian language it is you're interested in learning, and something about "learning better from females," or immediately asking email respondents "are you a guy or a girl?" (my email account back then used my Chinese name, which is not obviously female to a non-Chinese-speaker).

Although language learning itself is often seen as a lifelong endeavor, seeking language exchange -- with language learning perhaps only a tertiary goal -- becomes a bit creepy when you're over about forty. The assumed audience for language exchange is university-aged women. And although perfect Asian women only love older men and aren't concerned at all about the creep factor of an elderly man who wants to "practice Chinese," ignorant philistine bystanders might call the cops. So as fertile as language exchange is, it becomes less viable once you're over forty, at least in the Western world.

Don't panic. Expressing your Asian fetish still won't be too difficult after you're forty, even absent language exchange.

You might initially have the idea to volunteer as an English teacher, or a welcomer of immigrants, in your local community center or other organization. That might sound good, until you realize that any community center is most likely run by man-hating liberal feminists who will not appreciate your generous offers to provide your students extra tutelage in your home, or your offers to teach them the English terminology they might need if they seek to become board-certified urologists.

The answer is simpler than that. And it lies in your workplace. There have to be some Asian or part Asian or black-haired people somewhere in your office. Do your best to get near that person. Steer the conversation to Asia. Express your admiration. For example, if your fellow fry cook says you made the oil too hot, you might want to say, "speaking of hot, do you have a sister?" Or a more subtle approach: "speaking of oil, does your home country have oil reserves?"

A male friend of mine from business school is of Japanese ethnicity, and works in commercial loan underwriting. In his workplace, several times, he's noticed coworkers -- not direct coworkers, but people around him in the organization -- awkwardly try to get near him and get to know him and befriend him. Always white, always male. Initially, he thought either they really needed a friend at work -- which was strange, because they had many other coworkers who were closer to them -- or that they were gay and romantically interested in him -- which is not unthinkable, as he's a handsome devil. After a few "Hey Kenchi, want to go out for lunch together tomorrow?" offers from work acquaintances, the knew the pattern. "Yeah, I'm really, *really* interested in Japan. So... can you introduce me to any Japanese girls?" Not a bad strategy. After all, any ethnically Japanese man carries with him, in addition to his katana sword, a little black book of virginal Japanese swimsuit models (or better yet, hardcore porn stars) who are desperately single and wanting to date a divorced middle-aged accountant who hasn't had a date since the Koizumi administration. When Kenchi awkwardly told them that umm uhh not really, but he'll keep an eye out, the lunch invitations and desk-side chats ended. Other than the occasional, "so, got any Japanese ladies for me yet?" update requests.

That's the indirect method. And I don't want to bore you with a chronology of what I've seen of the direct method in the workplace. Including direct assertions, in an "as everybody already knows" tone, that Chinese girls don't have hangups. You know, hangups about sex with coworkers, bosses, subordinates, everybody. Or that Chinese girls are not so unreasonably obsessed with age as to worry about a man being thirty years older than me. Or that one day, they hope to retire and move to China (presumably with me, because I'd emigrated to America... in order to eventually move back to China with an elderly American man?), where life is just peachy, without any of the stress and other annoyances of American life.

It is cute that simultaneously to believing that I don't have "hangups" and that I will fuck anything cucumber-shaped, my male coworkers always feel the need to laboriously explain to me any slightly sexual or risque jokes, as if I, a thirtysomething-year-old woman living in

New York and having worked for almost a decade in a male-dominated office, had never heard of such things.

Taking your Asian fetish on the road

Asian fetishes, like Wrangler jeans, are much more popular in Asia than in the U.S. Exactly as is the case with Wrangler jeans, what will get you laughed at in the wrong crowd of Asian-Americans will get you adored and accepted in a crowd of Asians in Asia. "Wow, this guy is so interested in Asia," as we initially thought about our teacher Mr. G, before we started noticing how blatantly wrong most of his ideas of China were. You can go into a hip gathering place in Shanghai or Singapore or Tokyo and announce to everyone "I really love Asian culture," and there will be zero sniggering! Try that in the Western world! Is it any wonder that advanced Asian fetishists almost universally proceed to explore Asia?

As was the case with Mr. G, perhaps in your home country no one appreciates you, least of all the Subaru-driving, Tumblr-posting bull dykes who call themselves Western women. Perhaps in your home country, the liberal feminist educational mafia has deemed that your three years as a Walmart stock clerk don't qualify you to be a high school English teacher. Those same liberal feminists might have rejected your romantic advances for the decidedly unromantic reason of your lack of an income. Or maybe feminism has so consumed your country's legal system that a court is making you pay child support for your seldom-cooking ex-wife's mongrel spawn. Don't worry. Asia awaits. It is a vast, virginal expanse of virgin land and sea, longing for you to land and explore.

In Asia, there is no materialism, and you will be respected solely because of your gentlemanly virtues. Feminism is unheard of, and women busy themselves making sandwiches, or cooking chop suey, when they're not giving mind-blowing deep-throat testicle-tonguing fellatio to their boyfriends, husbands, and subway seatmates.

As you proceed to the higher levels of Asian fetishism, you will notice that Asian lands and people, like Asian foods, do have some heterogeneity. Chop suey, after all, tastes a little bit different from bulgogi, at least at better Asian buffets. And similarly, not all Asians from the Asian smorgasbord are exactly the same. Don't worry. I'm not suggesting that Asians are individuals or even that Asian culture from one country is vastly different from Asian culture from other countries. That would be madness! I'm only suggesting that there is some slight difference in the form of delectable pure hangup-free Asian-ness between Asians from different places -- and that to properly cultivate, celebrate, and enable your Asian fetish at the higher levels of development, you should be well aware of those differences.

You might have already guessed from the way I shat on Edward Said: I'm not one for long, nuanced, detailed academic explanations (other than when I'm being inscrutable in the bedroom). I prefer to get right to the point, at least when advising you about your Asian fetish.

The following is a list of all the countries in the Orient, with notable tips for practicing your Asian fetish when you're there:

China: Ancient, mysterious Chinese culture is primarily concerned with fake handbags, fake iphones, and fake orgasms. After 40,000 years as a strong and unified culture and society, we Chinese even built a wall to keep out foreigners and keep in the juices of delicious General Tso chicken. Because China is a communist society, capitalism is unheard of, money is an alien concept, and greed is deeply frowned upon. To impress a Chinese girl with your Asian fetish, it's best to assure her that you are not at all interested in money, property, or material advancement.

Taiwan: With its golden palaces, raucous night markets, spicy cuisine, and ping-pong-ball shows, Taiwan has long been a favorite destination for Asian fetishists drawn to the innate exoticism of its sun-kissed, golden brown, always-willing Asian culture. To seduce a Taiwanese girl, take her on a date to the Full Moon Party. And watch out for ladyboys.

Korea: Korea is a strong candidate to play host to the Asian Fetish World Congress because its population consists entirely of 23-year-old 5'8" women with D size breasts. In fact, in Korea, this look is so commonplace that K-pop starlets are considered ugly, which is why they always pout. Once you marry into a Korean family, even your grandfather-in-law will have a banging ass and legs, legs, legs up to here! Note of warning: Korean women are known for mutilating their Asian fetish-friendly small double-lidded eyes into big, round, single-lidded eyes that may uncomfortably remind you of the white vaginamonsters you left back home.

Vietnam: Vietnam was founded in the late 1960s, and is at war. When not fighting a war or listening to GWAR, the Vietnamese cultivate lemongrass, wear long flowing skirts, and take seductively furtive glances at French gentlemen. Vietnamese women are delicate lotus flower bamboo jasmine blossoms. Alongside constant war, Vietnam has embraced communism, so if you want to attract a Vietnamese woman, assure her that you don't have any money.

Japan: Japan is heaven on earth, a land where every girl is a teenager, every manga is a hentai, every bento is a sushi, and every car is a GT-R. A Japanese girl's typical fear of foreign men is that their taste in Japanese pornography is just not extreme enough. If you are well-developed enough in your Asian fetish to travel abroad, your taste in Japanese pornography must have long ago moved beyond vanilla. Assuage Japanese women's fears early, by not only telling them but actually showing them just how *extreme* your Japanese porn collection is. "Scat" in Japanese is "kuso," and that should be hello.

Thailand-Philippines: The nation of Thailand-Philippines has a storied history as the country where your divorced uncle likes to travel for some bullshit excuse you pretend to believe. The Oriental darlings of Thailand-Philippines are perpetually happy, but also very discerning, and this is why they are so eager to marry only the most senior Asian fetishists. Their perpetual happiness and smiles mean that greed is unheard of, so your uncle is absolutely safe trusting his new wife with his life insurance policy. If you aren't old enough to automatically say "Oriental" instead of "Asian," you haven't yet earned your wings to visit Thailand-Philippines.

Anywhere you go, whether the steppes of Shanghai or the transsexual bars of Thailand-Philippines, you are likely to be congratulated on your Asian fetish. Finally, you will be appreciated, whether it's while riding a rickshaw through Shanghai or katana-fighting in Tokyo or machine-gunning the enemy in Hanoi. And perfect specimens of Oriental femininity will flock to you. Because, as you have always known, and as your travels in Asia will definitely prove to you, Asian men are horrible neutered sexless macho weakling wife-beating guileless math geniuses, and once you appear on the scene, those Asian men will run away in fright.

Enjoy your time in Asia, but have an eye on the end-game. If repeated nightly encounters with Asian culture drain your funds, you may want to take up residence in the Asian branch office of Asian fetishism: English-language schools. Teaching English in Asia provides you with several of the prerequisites of Asian fetishism, including a low-paying job, a visa to an Asian country, and an endless parade of underage Asian femininity. It has been estimated that at least 130% of the foreigners teaching English in Asia have Asian fetishes. And what's the end-game here? You can marry one of your students, but that might be frowned upon by the authorities. The much better option: get nudes. Snapchat. You know the drill. Or if that's too difficult, download some nudes online and claim they're your students' nudes. Make sure to point out how this sort of thing is totally normal in Asia.

Once you've been fire -- oops, "not had your contract renewed" as an English teacher, you have three choices. You can become an expat, move to a new country, or put your tail between your legs and return to your home country. The first option is to seek a white-collar expat position with a major corporation, of the sort that comes with a gated villa, a bulletproof car, and a bedroom already stocked with almond-eyed concubines for your convenience. Insofar as expat positions are unavailable to those who have ever taught English, this is a realistic option only if you have read the previous few paragraphs of this book without actually having taken action on them. If so, congratulations. You are qualified to become an expat. If you did actually become an English teacher when reading the past few paragraphs, the joke's on you, kind of, because your lifespan as an Asian fetishist in Asia is somewhat limited, perhaps as limited as your parents' willingness to send you money. But don't worry. You can always take option two, which is moving on to the next country to claim as your own, generally in a pattern of decreasing GDP and increasing exoticism. In your new country, make sure to complain that the previous one "wasn't the real Asia" and the women there were all materialistic bull dyke bitches. Lather, rinse, repeat. Most importantly, no matter what you actually did in Asia, when you come back to your country, amaze them with tales of your expat package, and wistfully comment "and ah, the women there, man…" -- and everyone around will know exactly what you mean. You might even encourage some new Asian fetishes to develop.

Conclusion: ensuring a long and healthy Asian fetish

Few lifestyles are as vaunted, valuable, and celebrated as the Asian fetish lifestyle. Maybe you didn't choose the Asian fetish lifestyle, but it chose you. It doesn't matter, handsome man. You still have to actively maintain your fetish, lest it become rusty and not quite up to standard.

One quite notorious danger for the long-term Asian fetishist is that extended exposure to Asian people will cause the fetishist to unfairly conclude that Asians are no different from anyone else. Well, extended exposure to mercury also makes people go crazy, right? This is particularly pronounced among those fetishists who marry an Asian woman and come to suspect that her vagina isn't horizontal after all and she eats more than just flied lice. The nice thing about the methods in this book is they're universal. Even if you're living with a supposedly Asian woman in Sometown USA, you can firmly know and even promote and advocate the idea that things would be so much better if you moved to Asia, and got another, usually younger specimen.

The "no true Scotsman" method is quite helpful here. After discovering that the Asian woman you married farts, shits, and likes expensive handbags, you should properly conclude that she's not really Asian, that either you got "one of the bad ones," or she's been "Americanized" or "corrupted by feminism." And that things are so much better with the pure, uncorrupted, darling, virginal Asian specimens. And just follow the steps in my book.

In general, following this method should ensure a healthy Asian fetish well to the end of your natural lifespan. Witness the American men in New York who are on their fourth or fifth mainland-Chinese wives, claiming that the previous ones were "bad choices" or "Americanized" and that pure blissful sandwich-making perfection lies for them just over in the next Chinese village where they hunt (the big cities in China are, of course, too full of hirsute feminists -- just look at me!). Or look at those who make entire careers of their Asian fetishism, such as travel writers who can never stop crowing about the mystic exoticism of whatever Asian destination they're visiting, and inevitably wistfully concluding that one day they want to live the idyllic life of a Fujianese shrimp fisherman or a Burmese shit-shoveler or some such.

Most of all, your Asian fetish demands respect. Embrace it. Be it. I'll always be watching out for you with my inscrutable almond eyes, when I'm not busy brushing my silken black hair, making you sandwiches, or shooting razors out of my slanted vagina.